DATE DUE

FEB 2 8 1998		
APR 1 2 1999	MAY 0 7 2013	
DEC - 9 1999		
	MAY 1 8 2017	
MAY 1 8 2000	JUN 0 8 2017	
JUN 2 2 2000		
NOV 1 3 2000		
NOV 1 3 2000		
MAR 2 6 2003		
APR 4 2003		
MAY 1 7 2003		
APR 0 7 2007		
FEB 0 9 2008		
JUN 0 6 2008		
NOV 0 4 2010		

Demco, Inc. 38-293

TURKEY

Between East and West

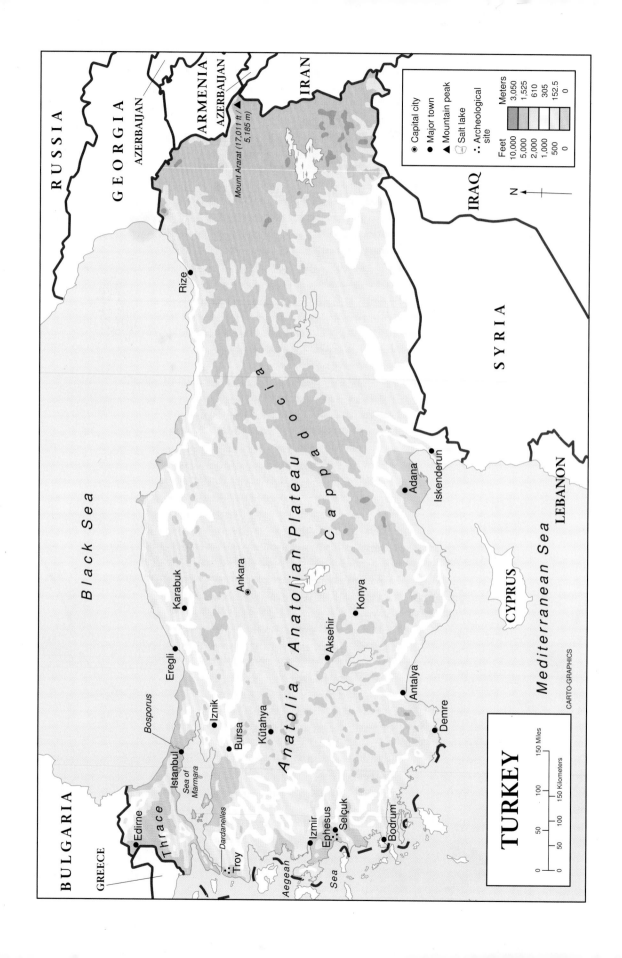

TURKEY

RUSSIA

GEORGIA

ARMENIA

AZERBAIJAN

AZERBAIJAN

IRAN

Mount Ararat (17,011 ft / 5,185 m)

BULGARIA

GREECE

Thrace

Black Sea

Rize

Edirne

Istanbul

Sea of Marmara

Bosporus

Eregli

Karabuk

Iznik

Bursa

Dardanelles

Kütahya

Ankara

Anatolia / Anatolian Plateau

Cappadocia

Aksehir

Konya

Adana

Iskenderun

IRAQ

SYRIA

Troy

Izmir

Ephesus

Selçuk

Bodrum

Aegean Sea

Antalya

Demre

CYPRUS

LEBANON

Mediterranean Sea

CARTO-GRAPHICS

	Capital city
	Major town
▲	Mountain peak
	Salt lake
∴	Archeological site

Feet	Meters
10,000	3,050
5,000	1,525
2,000	610
1,000	305
500	152.5
0	0

N

0   50   100   150 Miles

0   50   100   150 Kilometers

EXPLORING CULTURES OF THE WORLD

TURKEY

Between East and West

Louise R. Miller

BENCHMARK BOOKS

MARSHALL CAVENDISH

NEW YORK

The author thanks Kathryn Ece Ozyurt and Aydin Nurhan of the Turkish Consulate in Chicago, Illinois, for information and their generous review of the manuscript. The publisher would like to thank Fakhreddin Azimi, Associate Professor of History at the University of Connecticut, for his expert review of the manuscript.

Benchmark Books
Marshall Cavendish Corporation
99 White Plains Road
Tarrytown, New York 10591-9001

© Marshall Cavendish Corporation 1998

Library of Congress Cataloging-in-Publication Data
Miller, Louise R.
    Turkey: between east and west / Louise R. Miller
        p.   cm. — (Exploring cultures of the world)
    Includes bibliographical references (p.   ) and index.
    Summary: Discusses the history, geography, daily life, culture, and customs of the country that lies in both Asia and Europe.
    ISBN 0-7614-0397-3 (lib. bdg.)
    1. Turkey [1. Turkey.] I. Title. II. Series.
DR440.M55   1998
956.1—dc21

97-11536
CIP
AC

Printed in Hong Kong

Series design by Carol Matsuyama

Front cover: A Turkish woman in traditional dress
Back cover: Two girls pose among Roman ruins

Photo Credits
Cover: ©Steve Vidler/Leo de Wys, Inc.; back cover: ©Siegfried Tauquer/Leo de Wys, Inc.; title page and pages 29, 30, 36, 54, and 56: ©James L. Stanfield/National Geographic Society Image Collection; page 6: AP/Wide World Photos, Inc.; pages 9, 11, 14, 33, 43, and 48: ©Brent Peters; pages 10, 26-27: ©Miwako Ikeda/International Stock Photo; page 12: ©Ingeborg Lippman/Peter Arnold, Inc.; page 16: ©Giraudon/Art Resource, NY; pages 19 and 39: ©Oldrich Karasek/Peter Arnold, Inc.; page 20: ©Burhan Ozbilici/AP/Wide World Photos, Inc.; page 22: ©Robert Mackinlay/Peter Arnold, Inc.; page 28: ©Kadir Kir/International Stock Photo; page 35: ©Peter Langone/International Stock Photo; page 37: ©Richard T. Nowitz/National Geographic Society Image Collection; pages 40 and 53: ©Michele and Tom Grimm/International Stock Photo; pages 46-47: ©DeWys/Sipa/Rasmussen/Leo de Wys, Inc.; page 50: ©Michael Girard/International Stock Photo; page 51: ©Jeff Greenberg/Peter Arnold, Inc.; page 52: ©Gordon Grahan/National Geographic Society Image Collection.

Contents

Atatürk, the "Father of the Turks," freed the country from foreign rule and made Turkey a republic.

1
GEOGRAPHY AND HISTORY

The Birth
of a Republic

The "Father of the Turks"

The year was 1919. World War I was finally over, and the six-hundred-year-old Ottoman Empire had been defeated. It was about to be divided up between the victorious allies, Britain, France, and Italy. Turkey—the center of the empire—had already been invaded by Greek troops eager to claim their share of the spoils. It looked as if the Turks would no longer have a country to call their own.

At this moment of national crisis, a new leader arose. His name was Mustafa Kemal. Even when he was a boy, he was so bright and energetic that everyone thought he was destined for greatness. A mathematics teacher gave him the name Kemal, which means "perfection," to add to his given name, Mustafa.

Mustafa Kemal was determined to win Turkey's independence. He went on a whirlwind tour of the country, organizing an army and promoting nationalism. His countrymen responded. Often dressed in rags and armed with old weapons, they defeated the Greeks. On October 29, 1923, General Kemal declared Turkey an independent nation.

Mustafa Kemal became Turkey's first president. He wanted all Turks to take pride in their new nation. "Happy is he who calls himself a Turk," he repeated. Turks were *proud of their nation and of their leader. They revered Mustafa Kemal as a* ghazi, *or hero. In 1934, he was given a new name by the Turkish Grand National Assembly: Atatürk, Father of the Turks. That was how Mustafa Kemal Atatürk became the greatest* ghazi *in Turkey's long and amazing history.*

Fascinating Landscapes

Atatürk's love of Turkey may have had something to do with the physical beauty of the land. Turkey lies in two continents: Europe and Asia. The country's shape reminds some people of a buffalo. The buffalo's small head lies in the west, in Europe, and its large body lies in the east, in Asia. The European, or western, section of Turkey is part of a region called Thrace. The Asian, or eastern, area of Turkey is called Anatolia.

Turkey is a sprawling, mountainous land, about as large as the states of Texas and Tennessee combined. It has many neighbors: Greece to the west; Bulgaria to the northwest; Georgia, Armenia, Azerbaijan, and Iran to the east; and Iraq and Syria to the south. Turkey is also bordered by the Black Sea to the north, the Mediterranean Sea to the south, and the Aegean Sea to the west. With all these bodies of water, Turkey has many miles of sparkling coastline.

The Black Sea and the Mediterranean are linked by three narrow but important bodies of water, called the Straits—the Bosporus, the Sea of Marmara, and the Dardanelles. The Straits have had great political importance throughout history. Only by passing through them can Russian ships reach the Mediterranean to trade with the countries of northern Africa and southern Europe.

The unusual white terraces at Pamukkale, in southwestern Turkey, were carved out of the cliff by hot springs that contain a white mineral called calcium carbonate.

The Straits also separate Thrace and Anatolia. Although Thrace represents only 3 percent of the country, it contains its largest and best-known city, Istanbul (once called Constantinople). Thrace's gently rolling countryside is famous for its sweet melons, vineyards, and olive and fig trees.

The Turkish capital, Ankara, lies on a high, broad area of central Anatolia known as the Anatolian Plateau. Tall mountain ranges surround the plateau. Turks consider the plateau the "heartland" of their nation. Much of Anatolia is rugged and mountainous. One region, called Cappadocia, looks like

These ancient tombs were built into the cliffs along the coast of southern Turkey thousands of years ago.

the surface of the moon. The rocky landscape has been eroded into fantastic shapes by the wind and rain. People have carved unusual homes in the cavelike rocks.

Eastern Anatolia, a rocky and barren landscape, is known as the Wild East. It is where Turkey's highest mountain, Mount Ararat, rises 17,011 feet (5,185 meters) above sea level. According to the Bible, this is where Noah's Ark landed after the Flood.

Alive with Plants and Animals

Because of Turkey's geographical diversity, its countryside supports many types of plants and animals. Along the Mediterranean coastline, farmers grow grains, oranges and lemons, olives, and cotton. Deer and wild goats ramble among the hills, and birds fill the air with song.

The Black Sea coast is also fertile, producing large crops of cherries, hazelnuts, tea, and tobacco. Farmers on the dry Anatolian Plateau can grow little but wheat and barley. There

Bodrum, on the Aegean Sea, is dominated by the majestic ruins of a fortress built by the Crusaders—the Castle of St. Peter.

This man picks tea at one of the many plantations in Rize, Turkey's tea capital on the Black Sea.

and in eastern Anatolia, shepherds make a living raising sheep, just as their ancestors did. Huge dogs wearing spiky metal collars protect the sheep from the wolves and bears that live in the mountains.

Since Turkey covers such a broad range of territory, its climate is varied. In Thrace and along the Mediterranean coast, winters are mild and rainy, and summers are hot and dry. The Black Sea coast receives the most annual rainfall. The interior of Anatolia has cool, windy winters and hot, extremely dry summers.

A Look Back Through Time

Turkey has a long and rich history. The earliest human settlements there date back some 9,500 years. About 3,800 years ago, a people known as the Hittites arose. They created a powerful civilization that lasted about a thousand years, from 2200 B.C. to 1200 B.C. Later groups of people who moved to Anatolia also left their mark. Among them were the Phrygians, the Lycians, and the Lydians.

One character of Phrygian legend is Gordius. He tied a knot that was so hard to undo it had to be cut. Even today, when people solve a difficult problem, we say that they have "cut the Gordian knot."

King Midas, ruler of the Phrygians about 2,700 years ago, was said to have had unusual powers. According to legend, everything he touched turned to gold. Even his own daughter became a golden statue when he gave her a loving hug. Now we say that people who know how to make money easily have the "Midas touch."

More Conquerors

The ancient Persians conquered the region in the 500s B.C. They were vanquished in turn by the famous Greek warrior Alexander the Great, in 334 B.C. Greek language and customs then flourished in the land. Two centuries later, the Romans invaded, and Turkey became part of the Roman Empire. More than 40,000 Greek and Roman ruins can be found throughout Turkey today.

In A.D. 330, the Roman emperor Constantine moved his court to the ancient Greek city of Byzantium on the Bosporus Straits. It was renamed Constantinople in honor of the emperor, who had converted to Christianity and made it the official religion of the empire. Then in 395, the entire Roman Empire was divided into two parts. The western part of the empire was centered in Rome. The eastern part, called the Byzantine Empire, was ruled from Constantinople.

Constantinople was the glittering heart of the eastern empire for nearly a thousand years. Its most enduring monument is the Hagia Sophia (Church of the Holy Wisdom), built in the sixth century by Emperor Justinian. Its huge, magnificent dome is a marvel of engineering.

The library of Celsus was part of the ancient Greek city of Ephesus, today one of the largest archaeological sites in the world.

The Turks Settle in Turkey

Over time, the Byzantine Empire grew increasingly corrupt and became vulnerable to attack. It was invaded by a group of nomads that arrived from central Asia in the A.D. 1000s. They were the Seljuk Turks. Fierce warriors, the Seljuk Turks fought for their faith, the religion of Islam. They rewarded their greatest warriors with the title of *ghazi*, hero of the faith. The Seljuk Turks battled the Byzantines for two hundred years and established the state of Rum in central Anatolia.

The Seljuk Turks were an artistic, deeply religious people. With them came an Islamic group called the Whirling Dervishes. These men worshipped by performing a rapid, spinning dance until they fell into a trance. Even today, we might refer to someone who seems to be in constant motion as a "whirling dervish."

The Ottoman Empire Begins

In the 1200s, Anatolia was invaded by another group of people from central Asia: the Ottoman Turks. Their sultan, or king, was named Osman. He began an era of strong rule, stability, and order. His descendants governed for six hundred years—until the end of World War I.

The Ottoman sultans expanded their territory until their authority extended over many lands and peoples. Probably the most famous sultan was Süleyman the Magnificent, who ruled from 1520 to 1566. Under his leadership, Turkish culture reached its high point. He was also a great conqueror. His thundering army struck fear into the heart of European Christendom. Süleyman led his troops deep into Europe; they were only stopped at the gates of Vienna.

Süleyman the Magnificent's invasion of Europe was stopped when the Turks failed to capture Vienna in 1529.

By the 1570s, the Ottoman Empire had reached its greatest extent. The sultan's rule stretched from Greece, the Balkans, and southern Russia in Europe; to Egypt, Algeria, Tunisia, and Libya in Africa; to Palestine, Iraq, and part of Arabia in the Middle East. The power and extent of the empire was vast. The authority of the sultan was so great that his subjects called him the "Shadow of God on Earth."

The Ottoman Empire grew immensely rich, and Turkish arts and crafts flourished. Turkish architecture was especially magnificent. The Turks became famous for their beautiful calligraphy (artistic handwriting), woodwork, tiles, and textiles. They are still known for these crafts today.

The "Sick Man of Europe"

The sultans lived in gigantic, luxurious palaces cut off from the rest of the world. They ruled their great empire through servants and knew little of life outside the thick palace walls. In the 1700s, the Ottoman Empire slowly began to decline. As the sultans lost control, other powerful empires arose, and they began to take over some Ottoman lands. In this weakened condition—in 1853 it was described by Nicholas I of Russia as the "Sick Man of Europe"—the Ottoman Empire allied itself with Germany before World War I.

Atatürk Shapes the Nation

Germany and the Ottoman Empire lost the war. The old empire had finally died—but what would replace it?

A young army general, Mustafa Kemal, had a vision for the future. He wanted to cast off the shadow of the empire and turn Turkey into a modern state. With a ragtag Turkish army, he fought for Turkish independence and won.

Atatürk was the president of the republic of Turkey for fifteen years. During that time, he made many changes in the way Turks were governed and educated. For the first time, he separated the laws of Turkish government from the rules of Islam. Islamic law has many rules governing the way people behave—from how they dress to the foods they eat. Atatürk wanted religion to be separate from the state.

Before Atatürk came to power, women had few rights in Turkey. A man, for example, was allowed to have more than one wife. Under the republic, all people—women as well as men—received the right to vote. And men could no longer have more than one wife. Atatürk also made primary education free for all children. The Ottoman Turkish language was a mixture of Persian, Arabic, Turkish, and European words. Atatürk eliminated many foreign words and changed the alphabet from Arabic to Latin characters.

New Clothes, New Names

Atatürk also wanted Turks to adopt Western dress. He ordered men to stop wearing the traditional fez, a brimless red felt hat with a flat top. The fez, Atatürk thought, was a symbol of the old empire. He introduced Western-style hats for men, and discouraged women from wearing veils, which were customary in Islamic lands.

Until Atatürk's rule, Turks did not have last names. Their one and only name was the same as that of millions of their countrymen—Mustafa, or Ahmet, or Hasan. There was no way for the government to tell one Mustafa or Ahmet or Hasan from the next. In 1934, the Grand National Assembly required all Turks to choose last names. As an example, the assembly chose a new name for the president: Atatürk.

18

These modern girls from Antalya, in southwestern Turkey, wear the traditional clothes of their region, including the fezes that Atatürk discouraged.

Turkey After Atatürk

Atatürk died in 1938, shortly before World War II began. Turkey did not take sides until nearly the end of the war, although it quietly helped countries that opposed Hitler. Then in 1945, Turkey declared war on Germany. Because it was on the winning side, Turkey became a founding member of the United Nations and joined the North Atlantic Treaty Organization (NATO), in 1952. During the 1950s and 1960s, Turkey was a strong ally of the United States and Western European countries against the Communist Soviet Union. In 1947, when

19

the Soviet Union demanded joint control of the Straits, the United States gave Turkey the military aid it needed to keep out the Soviets.

The Turkish road to democracy has been a rocky one. For centuries during the Ottoman Empire, the sultan's word was law. Even during the early years of the republic under Atatürk, there was only one political party, the Republican People's Party. After World War II, however, the Democratic Party was formed. In 1950 it won a majority in the Grand National Assembly. Unfortunately, within a few years, the party's leaders began to restrict freedom of speech and punish people who disagreed with them.

In 1960, Turkey's military leaders decided that Atatürk's idea of a republic was being threatened. They seized control of the government until a new Constitution was written. Turkey then returned to civilian rule. Since 1961, the military has

Former Prime Minister Necmettin Erbakan (right) *attends a government ceremony with his deputy, Tansu Ciller.*

TURKISH GOVERNMENT

Turkey is a republic. In this form of government, the president and other officials are elected by the citizens to carry out the law of the land. The present Turkish Constitution was adopted in 1982. It calls for a president, a prime minister, a cabinet, and a legislative body called the Grand National Assembly.

In Turkey, the president is the head of state and commander-in-chief of the military. He is elected for seven years by the Grand National Assembly, which is made up of 450 deputies elected by the voters. The Grand National Assembly can make laws, ratify treaties, and declare war.

The prime minister is head of government and is selected by the president. The prime minister in turn nominates members of the cabinet, whom the president then appoints. Choices for cabinet members, as well as new government programs, must be submitted to the Grand National Assembly for a vote of confidence.

Turkey's legal system includes the Constitutional Court, which decides whether a law passed by the assembly is legal. The Court of Cassation considers the decisions of lower courts, which are located throughout the country.

Turkey has 67 provinces, each with a governor appointed by the president. The council for each province is elected by the voters. The major political parties in Turkey are the True Path, the Welfare (*Refah*), and the Motherland parties.

stepped in twice more during periods of social and political unrest. Each time, a new Constitution has been adopted.

In the 1990s, a conflict developed in Turkish politics. The pro-Islamists want the nation to pay more attention to Islamic laws and customs and to have closer economic ties to other Islamic countries. Other people want Turkey to remain true to Atatürk's vision of a Westernized republic, one in which the rules of the state are separate from Islamic law. In June 1996, the two sides compromised; a new government was formed between the Welfare (pro-Islamist) Party and the True Path Party. The prime minister, Necmettin Erbakan, was a pro-Islamist, but he resigned in June 1997. The struggle between the two visions of Turkey continues.

These Kurdish shepherd boys guard their flocks on a plain below Mount Ararat, in eastern Turkey.

2
THE PEOPLE

Who Are the Turks?

Today the people of Turkey are a fascinating mixture of those who came before them. About 90 percent of the people can trace their ancestry to the Seljuk Turks and the Ottoman Turks. The rest belong to twenty-two different ethnic groups. The largest of these groups is the Kurds, who live in eastern Anatolia. Other minority groups include Arabs, Greeks, Armenians, Georgians, and Circasians.

How the Turks Worship

Almost 99 percent of the Turkish population are Muslims—followers of the religion of Islam. The rest are Orthodox Christians and Jews. Although Islam is the main religion, all faiths can be practiced freely in Turkey.

Muslims observe the teachings of the Prophet Muhammad, who lived from about A.D. 570 to A.D. 632 on the Arabian Peninsula. According to Islamic belief, Muhammad was the last in a long line of prophets, stretching from Abraham to Moses to Jesus, who received the revelations of God. Muhammad himself is not considered divine, but he taught people to believe that there is only one God ("Allah," in Arabic). Muhammad's teachings were later collected in a book called the Koran.

To be a good Muslim, one should obey the Five Pillars of Islam. First, Muslims need to profess their faith: "There is no god but Allah, and Muhammad is his prophet." Second, they should pray five times a day, facing in the direction of the holy city of Mecca, in Saudi Arabia. Chanters known as muezzin (moo-eh-ZEEN) call worshippers to prayer at dawn, noon, in the middle of the afternoon, at sunset, and at night. Third, Muslims should fast from sunrise to sunset each day during the month of Ramadan. Fourth, they should give money to the poor. Fifth, they should make a pilgrimage at least once in their lives to Mecca, where the holiest Muslim shrine is located and where Muhammad was born.

Mosques are Muslim places of worship. They usually consist of a large, square building topped by a dome. Tall, slender towers called minarets are attached to them. Muezzin call the faithful to prayer from the top of the minarets. Five times a day, the chanting of the muezzin can be heard all over Turkey.

The Language Says a Lot

The official language of Turkey is Turkish. However, other languages are also spoken. The Kurds speak Kurdish, and other groups speak Armenian, Arabic, or Greek. The Turkish language is related to both Finnish and Hungarian. Since Turks are a polite people, they use many expressions of courtesy. They also often use body language when they speak. For "yes," Turks say *evet* (EH-vet) and nod their heads forward and down. For "no," they say *hayir* (HI-yir) and nod their heads up and back. If Turks do not understand something, they shake their heads from side to side.

The Turkish alphabet has twenty-nine letters, with several accent marks and a dotless "i." Words are formed by adding endings to basic words. Sometimes the endings combine to make very, *very* long words—even as long as sentences! Since Atatürk simplified the language, however, many more people are able to read—no matter how long the words are.

City Life

About half the population of Turkey lives in cities. The largest city is Istanbul, with about twelve million residents. The second-largest city is the capital, Ankara. Other major cities are Izmir and Edirne.

The beautiful Süleymaniye Mosque, built between 1550 and 1557 by Sinan, the most famous Turkish architect of the time, rises above the city of Istanbul.

The cities are a fascinating mixture of the old and the new, Islamic and Western. Sixteenth-century mosques rise next to twentieth-century skyscrapers. Cars and buses zoom past plodding carts and donkeys. As in modern cities the world over, residents have jobs in manufacturing or in banking, as teachers or as computer operators. They can also work as shopkeepers in the ancient bazaars—as colorful now as they were three hundred years ago—or as carpet weavers or pipe makers.

Most industrial jobs can be found around cities. Turkey's major industries include shipbuilding, textiles, leather, iron, pharmaceuticals, and carpet making. Iron and steel plants are located in Karabuk, Eregli, and Iskenderun.

Starting in the 1940s, people from the countryside began to move to the cities in search of jobs. Informal communities were formed around the city outskirts. At first these communities were very poor. Gradually they improved, and people went from living in hastily built shacks to more comfortable, permanent dwellings. Today, wealthier residents may live in suburban homes or in

These men work at a shipyard, crafting wooden boats by hand.

concrete apartment houses. Still, most city dwellers live in crowded areas spread out on the hillsides surrounding every major Turkish city.

Country Life

Life in the villages of Anatolia is quieter and more traditional. Here farmers, shepherds, and cattle raisers still live according to the ancient rhythms of the land: planting, growing, harvesting. Villagers near the Black Sea may live in thatched-roof cottages, while those in central Anatolia often live in brick houses with flat roofs. Stone cottages still dot the landscapes of southern and western Anatolia.

What Do They Wear?

Atatürk's clothing laws of the 1920s transformed the dress of the Turkish people practically overnight. Men who had worn traditional red fezes and white bloomers suddenly dressed like Western businessmen, with suits and brimmed hats. Women, especially in the cities, began to wear Western-style dresses and coats.

Today the suits and dresses remain, along with blue jeans and sneakers. Traditional clothes can still be found, though, especially in villages. Women in the countryside often cover their heads and the lower part of their faces with colorful scarves or veils. Wearing a head covering is a traditional sign of modesty in Islamic cultures. In recent years, the full head veil has reappeared, even in cities. Some women and men still wear baggy trousers, called *salvar*, to which men add the traditional loose coat. Many Turks have folk costumes put away for special holidays, when they like to display their Turkish heritage.

Turkey's nomadic peoples, such as these Turkoman women, still wear traditional clothing.

This family belongs to the Honamli tribe, one of the few groups in Turkey that are still nomadic.

3

FAMILY LIFE, FESTIVALS, AND

All in the Family

Family ties are strong in Turkey. The father is the head of the household, and the mother has primary responsibility for the care of the children and the home. Often familes live in extended households, with three or four generations under one roof. Children have deep respect for their elders. Young people do not smoke, drink, argue, or speak rudely in the presence of older family members.

For centuries, the most important role for Turkish women was to bear a son. Before the 1920s, women were second-class citizens, always under the rule of their fathers, husbands, brothers, and sons. They could neither vote nor get a divorce. During the Ottoman Empire, a man could have more than one wife. The wives of noblemen lived with their children in a harem, a place in the palace set aside only for them.

Under Atatürk's rule, the laws were changed. Polygamy and arranged marriages were outlawed, and women received the right to vote and to get a divorce. Today more Turkish women are educated, and more work in professions. Old customs persist in rural areas, however. Many marriages are still arranged, and some men still take a second wife.

Children are treasured in Turkish society, and parents want their children to be well educated. Some children, however, have to work in addition to, or instead of, going to school. Village children have always helped in the fields. Today they continue to help with farm work, tend to the animals, or assist with household chores. They may even work at weaving the family carpet. In the cities, children often work in family restaurants or bazaars. Sometimes they labor long hours in factories, for less pay than adults.

Festivals and Holidays Are for Fun

When the work is done, Turks are ready to have a good time. They celebrate both national holidays and religious holidays. An important holiday is April 23, National Independence Day, the day on which the Grand National Assembly was founded in 1923. It is also Children's Day, because Atatürk wanted to honor children. Some holidays commemorate Atatürk's life. May 19 is Atatürk's birthday as well as National Youth and Sports Day. On November 10, the date of Atatürk's death, the Turks observe a moment of silence at 9:05 A.M., the exact time of his death.

Islam Celebrates

Turkey uses the Western calendar for government holidays. Religious holidays are celebrated according to the lunar calendar, which is used in the Islamic world. It is eleven days shorter than the Western calendar, so Islamic religious holidays do not fall on the same day every year.

Children accompany their mother as she sells her produce in an outdoor market.

Most Turks keep the fast during the month of Ramadan, as directed by the Koran, the Muslims' holy book. From sunrise to sunset, they allow nothing to pass their lips—no food, no drink, not even a cigarette or a postage stamp. At sunset, Muslim families enjoy a big meal to mark the end of the day's fast.

At the end of Ramadan, with the appearance of the new moon, Muslims celebrate the "festival that breaks the fast": *Eid al-Fitr*. This holiday lasts for three days. People visit family and friends. Children go from door to door asking for sweets. It's a happy time of year.

Another important holiday is *Eid al-Adha*, the Feast of the Sacrifice. It refers to the story of Abraham and Isaac. In Genesis 22, in the Bible, and Sura 37, in the Koran, Abraham almost sacrifices his son Isaac at God's request. At the last minute God saves Isaac by sending a ram to be sacrificed in his place. During the Feast of the Sacrifice, most Turkish families also kill a sheep. Well-off families donate meat to those who cannot afford a sheep of their own.

Music, Dance, and Wrestling

Many other festivals take place in different parts of Turkey throughout the year. These festivals highlight Turkey's diverse heritage.

In January, there is a camel-wrestling competition in Selçuk, a village in western Turkey. No, the camels don't actually wrestle, but they do shove and push each other around. People celebrate with folk dancing, parties, and concerts—even a beauty pageant for the camels!

In June, Istanbul hosts the International Arts Festival, a month-long celebration of dance, art, and music from all over

Camels are not only used for work; they also take part in festivals and even compete in beauty pageants!

the world. In August there is the Drama Festival in Troy. According to legend, this site along the Straits is where the Trojan War took place. The ancient Greek poet Homer told about the ten-year siege of Troy in his epic poem *The Iliad*. The siege ended when the Greeks hid warriors in a huge wooden horse and gave it as a gift to the city. Once the horse was inside the walls, the warriors came out and Troy was destroyed. Visitors to the Drama Festival can see a huge model of the wooden horse.

A Christian festival is held every December at the Church of St. Nicholas in Demre. St. Nicolas was a Byzantine bishop

Every December, the Whirling Dervishes of the Mevlevi order perform their ritual dance to honor their founder.

in the fourth century. When he was young, he performed many anonymous good deeds. One stormy night, so the story goes, he was secretly leaving some gold for a neighbor's daughter, who did not have a dowry. The door to her house was closed, so he dropped the gold down the chimney instead. Some of it fell in the girl's stockings, which were hung out to dry. So the legend of St. Nicholas—later known as Santa Claus—was born.

To finish off the year, Turks can go to the Rites of the Whirling Dervishes in Konya. Atatürk outlawed the dervishes when he modernized Turkey. Only once a year can Turks see them spin around in their spectacular, dizzying dances.

Tasty Turkish Treats

Turks are famous for their hospitality. They love to welcome visitors to their homes and proudly offer them a Turkish feast. Turkey has one of the most delicious cuisines in the world.

"May this be good for your health," a host may say to his guest. The meal that follows is usually very healthy, for Turks rely on natural foods from the Turkish countryside. There are olives and olive oil from olive trees, grapes and vine leaves

These men and women buy fresh tomatoes at a crowded, open-air market.

from local vineyards, goat cheese and yogurt from goat's milk, and home-grown vegetables like cucumbers and tomatoes. The most famous Turkish dish is probably shish kebab—lamb grilled on skewers with onions, tomatoes, and green peppers.

For breakfast, Turks might start the day with fresh bread, goat cheese, olives, and yogurt. Yogurt can be topped with confectioner's sugar or eaten plain. It can also be thinned out to make a liquid called *ayran* (eye-RAN). *Ayran* is a very popular drink in Turkey.

Lunch often consists of *dolmas*, which are vine or cabbage leaves stuffed with rice. Or it might be a delicious, healthy soup, like pumpkin or lentil soup. Turks eat a variey of vegetable soups.

Dinner may start out with several appetizers: chopped eggplant mixed with onion and garlic; bean salad; or yogurt mixed with grated cucumber and garlic. These will be followed by a main dish of lamb and rice or seafood. Fish and shellfish of many kinds—sea bass, swordfish, and turbot, mussels, crabs, and shrimp—are found in the coastal waters

DRIED APRICOT COMPOTE

Here's a simple, tasty dessert that people in Turkey often enjoy:

Ingredients:
    1/2 pound dried apricots
    4 cups water
    1 1/2 cups sugar

Put the apricots in a bowl with the water. Soak overnight. Transfer to a saucepan and add the sugar. Cover and simmer over low heat until the apricots are tender. Chill. Serves 4 to 6 people.

Döner kebabs, or gyros—delicious slices of barbecued lamb cooked on a rotating skewer—are a popular Turkish food.

off Turkey. Seafood grilled with lemon and parsley are a specialty of Istanbul and other coastal cities. Fish is rarely eaten by farmers in the central regions of Anatolia.

Finally comes the best part—the dessert. Turks love sweet, sugary foods of all kinds. One popular pastry, baklava (BAHK-lah-vah), is made with honey and nuts. Rice pudding, cold stewed fruit, and baked pumpkin and walnuts are also great favorites. With all the delicious possibilities, it is impossible to go away hungry from a meal in Turkey.

These boys, on a school outing in Istanbul, learn about their country's rich history.

4

SCHOOL AND RECREATION

Learning and Relaxing

Education has been important in Turkey ever since the nation's independence was declared in 1923. Atatürk wanted his countrymen to be prepared for the challenges of twentieth-century life. He closed religious schools and opened state schools, simplified the language by introducing the Latin alphabet, and set up the Ministry of Education. This ministry sets the standards for all schools.

Today, nearly every adult in Turkey can read. Literacy is still a problem in rural areas, however, where there aren't enough schools or teachers. Education is particularly important in Turkey today, because the population is booming. Half the population is younger than twenty years old. Many children will have to be educated and trained for the future.

Boys and girls start school at age six and must stay in school for at least five years, usually until they are eleven. During these years, Turkish children study arithmetic, geography, history, music, art, natural sciences, and the Turkish language. Throughout their years in school, Turkish children at all levels learn about civic responsibility and political

41

awareness. This is part of the pride Turks have in their country. On Monday mornings and Friday afternoons, the students sing the national anthem—to begin and end the week.

Discipline and respect for others are crucial to all children's education. When teachers walk into the classroom, the children stand up and greet them. Teachers have an important role in their pupils' behavior outside as well as inside the classroom. They even have a say in which television shows children may watch and when they should go to bed. Teachers are also allowed to tweak boys' ears or pull girls' hair if they misbehave in class. A common punishment is to stand in the corner.

The middle school program, for students from ages twelve to fourteen, is also compulsory. Many children in rural areas do not attend, however. Middle schools are few and far between, and young people are often needed to work on farms.

Test Time

Competition is fierce for a place in the country's 1,300 public high schools. For one prestigious secondary school in 1987, more than 4,000 students took entrance examinations for only 300 places!

The subjects in the *lise*—the college preparatory schools—are more advanced than those in primary schools. Students may take courses in chemistry, history, foreign languages, physics, natural sciences, Turkish language and literature, music, art and design, and physical education. Other secondary schools offer courses in domestic science, agriculture, or technical training, in which work skills and productivity are important. Religious schools have made a comeback in the 1990s. Ten percent of high school students enroll in Muslim teacher-training schools.

After three years of secondary school, students can make some choices. They can enter vocational schools for special job training. They can go to work. Or, they can enter a university. Turkish students can choose from more than twenty-five universities. The University of Istanbul, founded in 1933, is Turkey's largest, with more than 30,000 students. Nine universities were founded in Turkey in the 1980s, which shows how important education is to the Turks.

When Children Play

Turkish children have between two and three hours of homework a night. They are not busy with schoolwork or other chores all the time, however. Like children the world over, they find time to play games and have fun.

Turkish children have fun on their backyard playset.

RING GAME

Here's a circle game that can be played indoors or outdoors and with any number of people. Players need only a long string and a ring. The string has to be long enough to go around the circle of players. First, the ring is put on the string, and then the string is tied at the end to form a circle. Players sit in a circle, each one holding on to the string. The player who is "it" sits in the middle.

The point of the game is to pass the ring around the string without letting "it" know where it is. Players pretend to have the ring when they really don't. As they play, the players chant:

> Come, ring. Go, ring. Where is the ring?
> Here's the ring. The ring came. It went.
> Where is the ring? *Here* is the ring.

The player who is caught with the ring becomes "it," and the original "it" becomes a player. The game is over whenever the players decide to stop.

Turkish games are very old and usually involve just simple equipment—stones, coins, rings, scarves, sticks, chalk, or a jump rope. Children in villages and cities alike enjoy playing circle games, in which players form either single or double circles and somebody becomes "it." Losers often have to perform stunts or make funny animal noises.

Schools have organized team sports as well. Students may participate in basketball, volleyball, or soccer, among others. The most popular sport in Turkey, as in most of the world, is soccer, which the Turks call football. Every school, every empty street or vacant lot, has a soccer game going on most afternoons. Whenever a professional team plays, the streets close to the stadium are jammed in every direction.

Children in cities also like to watch television, play video games, or go to the movies. In rural areas, there may be just one or two televisions per village, and no movies for hundreds of miles. In these places, children rely more on traditional Turkish games.

When Everyone Plays

Adults, too, need time for relaxation. Family outings are a favorite pastime for young and old alike. Sundays are the best time to go to a town park for a picnic and a swim.

In cities and villages all over Turkey, men gather at the local coffeehouse to meet friends and discuss current events over a cup of steaming hot tea or coffee. Traditionally, women do not socialize with men in public places. Only in cities will women sometimes join the men in restaurants or coffeehouses.

Walking is for the whole family. On warm summer evenings, townspeople come out to stroll through the streets and greet friends and neighbors. Sometimes they might watch a dancing bear, moving to the music of a tamborine. Or they might listen to a musician play Turkish music on the *saz*, a stringed instrument like a banjo.

Turks enjoy watching and playing many of the same sports that we do—basketball and tennis, car racing, and horse racing. Some special spectator sports have been enjoyed for centuries. One ancient game is called *cirit* (JI-rit). Riders on horseback catch javelins—slender spears—that are thrown at them as they gallop past each other. *Cirit* is a winter sport played mainly in the eastern mountains. Then there's greased wrestling. The wrestlers wear black leather pants and put olive oil on their bodies to make them slippery.

The contestants wrestle until one pins the other by the shoulders. Yearly tournaments are held in Edirne, a city northwest of Istanbul, as they have been for six hundred years.

Each region in Turkey has its own type of sports. In Cappadocia, in central Anatolia, people ride horses through ancient cave dwellings. Further east they can try their luck at hiking or skiing down snow-covered mountains.

Swimming is a favorite activity along the hundreds of miles of Turkish coastline. Sports such as waterskiing and windsurfing are available on the Mediterranean and Aegean coasts. Rafters brave the white water on rivers near the Black Sea. No matter where in Turkey someone is born—on the coast, near the mountains, or by the rivers—there are lots of recreational possibilities.

Beaches are plentiful along Turkey's Mediterranean coast, where bathers can swim in the beautiful water through November.

Many of the rooms in Istanbul's Topkapi Palace are elaborately decorated with gold paint and mosaic tile.

5
THE ARTS

An Architectural
Treasure Chest

With its many ornate mosques, stately buildings, and beautiful museums, Turkey delights both young and old. Istanbul alone contains amazing architectural treasures.

The Topkapi Palace was the sultan's headquarters during the Ottoman Empire. Vast and complex, it was once home to 5,000 people. The harem—women's and children's quarters—alone contains 500 separate rooms and apartments. In the sultan's rooms, one can see the magnificence for which the empire was known—gold furniture and woodwork, jeweled fabrics, and priceless rugs.

Istanbul also contains two of the most famous religious buildings in the world, one Christian, one Muslim. The Hagia Sofia, the Church of the Holy Wisdom, is probably the greatest work of Byzantine architecture. It was built of marble from Egypt, ivory from Asia, and columns from classical Greek temples. It was turned into a mosque when the Ottomans conquered Constantinople in 1453. Today, the four-acre building is a museum.

The Blue Mosque is one of the most magnificent works of Muslim architecture. It gets its name from the 20,000 or so glazed blue tiles on the walls of its interior. The tiles are painted in a profusion of beautiful designs. Intricate geometrical designs weave in patterns of flowers, trees, and animals.

The Turkish Bazaar

Every Turkish town has its bazaar, or street market. The biggest one is in Istanbul. It is covered over, like an early version of a shopping mall, with sixty-five streets and about five thousand shops.

Istanbul's Grand Bazaar contains thousands of shops, which have a huge selection of items.

Bazaars are where you can find many traditional Turkish arts and crafts. The shops are loaded with carpets, copperware, bronzeware, gold jewelry, ceramics, silks, shawls, and spices. There is an art to shopping in a bazaar. First the merchant will quote a price, about ten times what the item is worth. Then the shopper comes back with a price about one-tenth of what it is worth. Merchant and shopper negotiate until a compromise is reached. In the end, both feel they've struck a good bargain.

Magic Carpets

The most prized Turkish craft is carpet making. The art of the carpet goes back a thousand years, to the eleventh century and the Seljuk Turks.

The Seljuk Turks were originally nomads who lived in tents and mud-brick huts. They put carpets on the ground and hung them from the walls to keep out the cold and damp. They even used them as blankets. Turks came to count their carpets, along with their animals and jewelry, as part of the family wealth. Young girls brought their carpet with them as part of their dowry when they married.

Every tribe had its own traditional carpet designs. The bold, bright patterns were inspired by objects in

A Turkish woman weaves a carpet in much the same way as her ancestors used to do.

the natural world, such as plants, sheep, camels, or snakes. Rugs today are still decorated with these traditional designs. Some rugs include designs that are used all over the Islamic world. Prayer rugs, for instance, have common symbols such as the Tree of Life or the mosque lamp.

51

Rug sellers show their products to passersby in a busy rug market in Konya.

Carpet making has always been a woman's art, passed from one generation to the next. Girls may start learning to weave at the age of seven. "Little hands tie tighter knots" is an old Turkish saying. Village women set up looms in their homes and weave with wool from the family's sheep or goats. It used to be that the carpets they made were just for their family's use. Today, however, women can make an important contribution to the family income by selling the carpets they weave to rug sellers.

Carpet making is also taught in school. A girl might work on a carpet for two years and then sell it. The money she earns goes to the school. When she graduates, she receives a loom and must teach one other person how to weave a carpet. That way, the tradition continues.

The best-known type of Turkish carpet is the *kilim* (kee-LEEM), a flat woven rug. Turks also weave knotted pile carpets. Some expert carpet makers are able to tie thirty knots a minute! The most luxurious carpets, known for their rich colors and fine details, are made of silk.

Carpet patterns all have special meanings. Merchants delight in telling the story behind every rug they sell—over a cup of sweet tea or coffee—to eager listeners.

A Rainbow of Crafts

Other ancient arts are still alive and well in Turkey. Pottery making, for instance, is a centuries-old tradition in Anatolia. Kütahya is known for plates and bowls decorated in soft blues, greens, and reds. Potters in Iznik make the blue tiles that adorn mosques such as the Blue Mosque in Istanbul, and

Copper and bronze trays, coffee pots, and other products fill a shop in the Grand Bazaar.

other public buildings. In Iznik, Istanbul, and Kütahya, students can take courses that keep the tradition of handmade pottery alive.

Much of the copper and bronze work sold in the bazaars is now made in factories. Master coppersmiths, however, still make fine trays, pots, and pipes in designs that go back a thousand years.

Songs and Dances Close to the Heart

Turkish music has many roots. Some folk music can even be traced back to the days of the Persian and Byzantine Empires. These are songs of love, wine, and loss, accompanied by flutes, zithers, and drums. The old strains of folk music can still be heard in the Turkish rock music of today.

This man plays a type of Turkish flute.

During the Ottoman Empire, many European musical influences were also felt. The sultan's Janissaries (soldiers) marched into battle to the beat of kettledrums and bagpipes. In the twentieth century, there has been a merging of Turkish music and European classical music. Using European forms, such as the symphony and the rhapsody, composers include Turkish rhythms or themes.

Traditional Turkish folk dances are still enjoyed throughout the country. Each region has its own dance and

THE HOÇA AND THE COOKING POT

One day the Hoça borrowed a cooking pot from a neighbor. When he returned it the next day, the big pot had a small pot nestled inside.

"But I lent you only one pot," the neighbor said, surprised.

"Your pot had a baby," the Hoça said.

The neighbor now had two pots instead of one, so he happily accepted the explanation. The next time the Hoça asked for the pot, the neighbor lent it to him again. But the following morning the Hoça returned without it.

"Where is my pot?" the neighbor demanded.

The Hoça shrugged. "I'm afraid your pot has died."

"That is ridiculous!"

"You believed that your pot had a baby," the Hoça answered him. "If you accept the fact of birth, you must also accept death."

its own costume. In the area around the Black Sea, men dressed all in black and silver perform a dance called the *Horon*. In Bursa, a region in northwestern Anatolia, men perform a wild, dramatic dance called the *Kilic Kalkan*, the Sword and Shield. Pretending to be Ottoman warriors, they stage a mock fight. Both men and women, outfitted in colorful costumes and holding two wooden spoons in each hand, perform the popular Spoon Dance.

Poetry, Plays, and Stories

Like other ancient lands, Turkey has a wealth of poetry, stories, and theater. As far back as the A.D. 700s, wandering minstrels sang songs of heroes, love, and death. Seljuk Turks passed down poems and legends about their nomadic wanderings.

Folktales have survived over the centuries, told and retold. The most popular tales are about the adventures of Nasrettin Hoça (*hoça* means "schoolteacher"). Hoça, who was

Traditional Turkish military music, called Janissary music, uses a variety of drums, as well as bells and cymbals.

probably a real person, lived in Aksehir, a town in central Turkey, about six hundred years ago. Many funny stories have been made up about him over the centuries. They are full of jokes, tricks, gossip, and everyday wisdom. Even today, Turks will start laughing at the mere mention of his name. Children learn Hoça stories as soon as they are old enough to read.

Shadow-puppet theater is another traditional art form that is still very popular with Turkish children. Puppet shows were introduced in Turkey during the early days of the Ottoman Empire. The puppets are made from colorfully painted, see-through animal skins and are projected onto a white screen. One of the main puppet characters is the clever Karagoz (CAR-eh-guzh), a rude man who uses his wit to outsmart his enemies. Sometimes he makes fun of the silly and stupid things that people do—just for laughs. And he gets them!

Modern Literature

In the 1800s and 1900s, Turkish writers produced realistic novels, plays, and poems that tell the story of their country. Many works emphasize patriotic themes, social justice, or everyday life. Mahmut Makal's *Our Village* (1950) tells about life in a remote Anatolian village. The hero of Yasar Kemal's *Mehmed, My Hawk* (1961) is a Turkish Robin Hood who defies injustice and helps the poor. Kemal has been nominated for the Nobel Prize in literature.

The most famous poet is Nazim Hikmet (1902–1963). His work is controversial in Turkey today because of his Communist beliefs. But experts agree that Hikmet was one of the foremost poets of the twentieth century. His poems, plays, and novels celebrate the War of Turkish Independence and explore Turkish life, past and present.

Turkish arts and crafts have survived for many centuries under many empires and rulers. Each generation has preserved traditional forms and values while adapting to contemporary themes. Master writers and potters, musicians and carpet makers, proudly continue to pass on their techniques and talents to Turkish children—who will become the artists of tomorrow.

Country Facts

Official Name: Türkiye Cumhuriyeti (Republic of Turkey)

Capital: Ankara

Location: in southeastern Europe and southwestern Asia; bordered on the west by Greece; on the northwest by Bulgaria; on the northeast by Georgia, Armenia, Azerbeijan, Iran; on the south by Iraq and Syria. The Black Sea is to the north, the Aegean Sea to the west, and the Mediterranean Sea to the west and south

Area: 300,948 square miles (779,452 kilometers). *Greatest distances:* east–west, 1,015 miles (1,633 kilometers); north–south, 465 miles (748 kilometers). *Coastline:* 2,211 miles (3,558 kilometers)

Elevation: *Highest:* Mount Ararat, 17,011 feet (5,185 meters). *Lowest:* sea level along the coast

Climate: winters range from cold on the central plateau to mild and rainy along the Mediterranean and Black Sea coasts. Summers are hot and dry along the western and southern coasts; mild along the northern coast; and hot, windy, and extremely dry in the interior of Anatolia

Population: 63,204,000 (1996). *Distribution:* 69 percent urban; 31 percent rural

Form of Government: republic

Important Products: *Agriculture:* cattle, fruit, nuts, tea, tobacco, corn, sugar, beets, cotton, olives, sheep, barley, wheat, goats, cereal grains. *Industries:* shipbuilding, food processing, textiles, leather goods, iron, pharmaceuticals, carpet making, cars, tobacco, small appliances. *Natural Resources:* bauxite, boron, coal, chromium, copper, iron ore, lead, magnesium, meerschaum, petroleum, zinc

Basic Unit of Money: lira; 1 lira = 100 kurus

Language: Turkish

Religion: 99 percent Islam; small Christian and Jewish groups

Flag: white crescent and five-pointed star on red background

National Anthem: *Istiklâl Marsi* ("Independence March")

Major Holidays: New Year's Day, January 1; National Independence Day and Children's Day, April 23; Atatürk's Birthday and National Youth and Sports Day, May 19; Victory Day, August 30; Republic Day, October 29; Moment of Silence, November 10; Ramadan, *Eid al-Fitr* ("Feast that Breaks the Fast") and *Eid al-Adha* ("Feast of the Sacrifice"), dates change from year to year according to the lunar calendar.

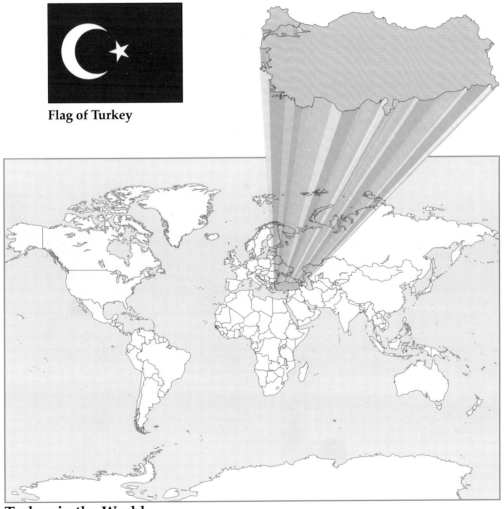

Flag of Turkey

Turkey in the World

Glossary

Allah (ah-LAH): the Arabic word for God

ayran (eye-RAN): a popular yogurt drink

baklava (BAHK-lah-vah): a sweet pastry made with honey and nuts

bazaar (bi-ZAHR): a marketplace for a wide variety of goods, with everything from copperware to food

calligraphy: beautiful, artistic handwriting

dowry: the money or property that a woman brings to her marriage

fez: a brimless hat with a flat top, usually red with a tassle

Gordian knot: a knot that cannot be untied

harem: the place set aside for women and children at the palaces of Ottoman sultans and noblemen

karagoz (CAR-eh-guzh): an important character in shadow-puppet theater

kilim (kee-LEEM): a type of Turkish carpet with flat-woven fibers

Koran (core-RAN): the sacred book of Islam

Midas touch: the ability to turn everything you touch to gold, based on the legend of King Midas

minaret (min-eh-RET): a tower attached to a mosque

mosque: an Islamic place of worship

muezzin (moo-eh-ZEEN): the person who calls Muslims to prayer five times a day

nomad: a member of a group or tribe that does not have a permanent home; nomads wander from place to place seeking food for themselves and their animals.

plateau: a high area of flat land

polygamy: marriage in which a man has more than one wife

prophet: a person who tells others a message that is believed to be from God

Ramadan (RAH-meh-dahn)**:** the Islamic month during which Muslims fast from sunrise to sunset each day

shish kebab: a popular lamb dish, with chunks of lamb and pieces of vegetables cooked on long skewers

sultan (SUL-tin)**:** the king of certain Islamic countries; during the Ottoman Empire, Turkey was ruled by sultans.

turban: a head covering that is made by wrapping a long strip of cloth around the head several times

Western: referring to people and customs from Europe and North America

Whirling Dervish: a member of an Islamic religious group who worships by dancing until he is in a trance-like state

For Further Reading

Algar, Ayla Esen. *The Complete Book of Turkish Cooking*. London: Kegan, Paul International, 1985.

Bell, Brian, editorial director. *Turkey* (Insight Guides). Singapore: APA Publications, 1995.

Bickman, Connie. *Children of Turkey*. Minneapolis, Minnesota: Abdo Consulting Group, Inc., 1994.

Dorson, Richard M., editor. *Folktales Told Around the World*. Chicago: The University of Chicago Press, 1975.

Feinstein, Steven. *Hero of Modern Turkey: Atatürk*. New York: Julian Messner, 1972.

Metin, And. *Karagoz Turkish Shadow Theater*. Evans, Nevada: Dost Publications, 1987.

Sheeban, Sean. *Turkey*. New York: Marshall Cavendish, 1993.

Spencer, William. *The Land and People of Turkey*. New York: J. B. Lippincott, 1990.

Walker, Barbara K. and Walker, Warren S. *Turkish Games for Health and Recreation*. Lubbock, Texas: Texas Tech Press, 1983.

Index

Page numbers for illustrations are in boldface

About the Author

Louise Miller has written four books for children and young adults. She has lived in Germany and Austria and is now a resident of Chicago.